A Note From Miracle Sims

This coloring book was inspired by the amazing Ladies of Unwine!

Unwine Self-Care and Sips Spa is a Facebook group and a movement created by yours truly as a reminder for ladies to take the time to take care of themselves, and Unwine! Yes, Un-Wine! (There's usually wine involved in some of my self-care routines)

"I hope that this coloring book inspires you to give yourself the well deserved "me time" we all desire! So grab a glass of wine and enjoy!"

"Miracle"

UNWINE

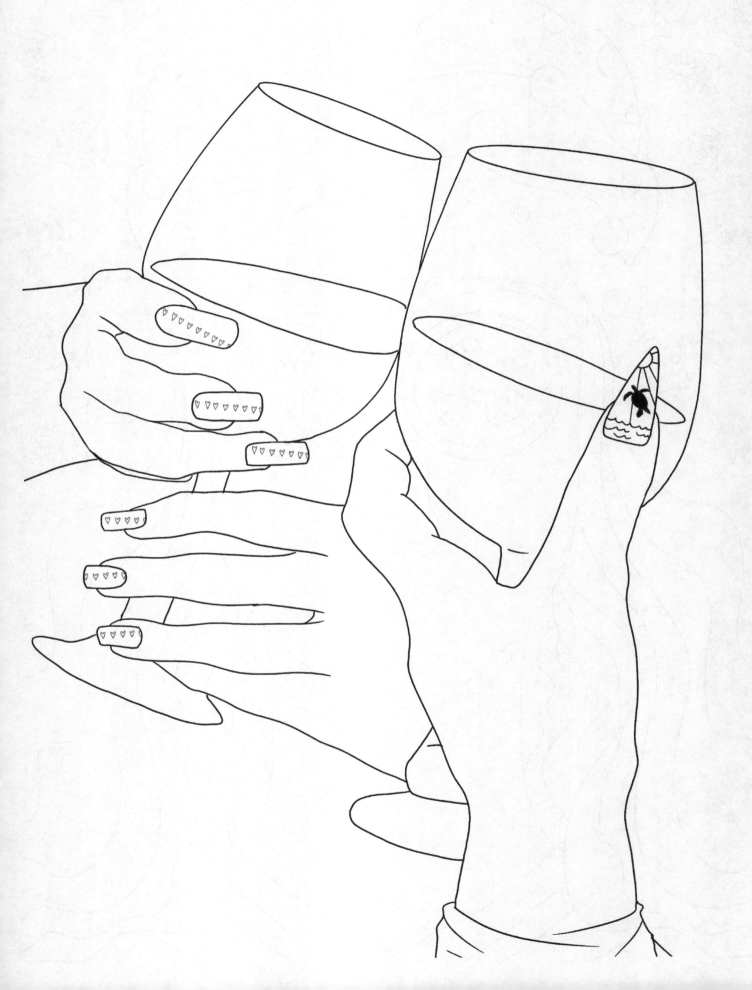

I am beautiful

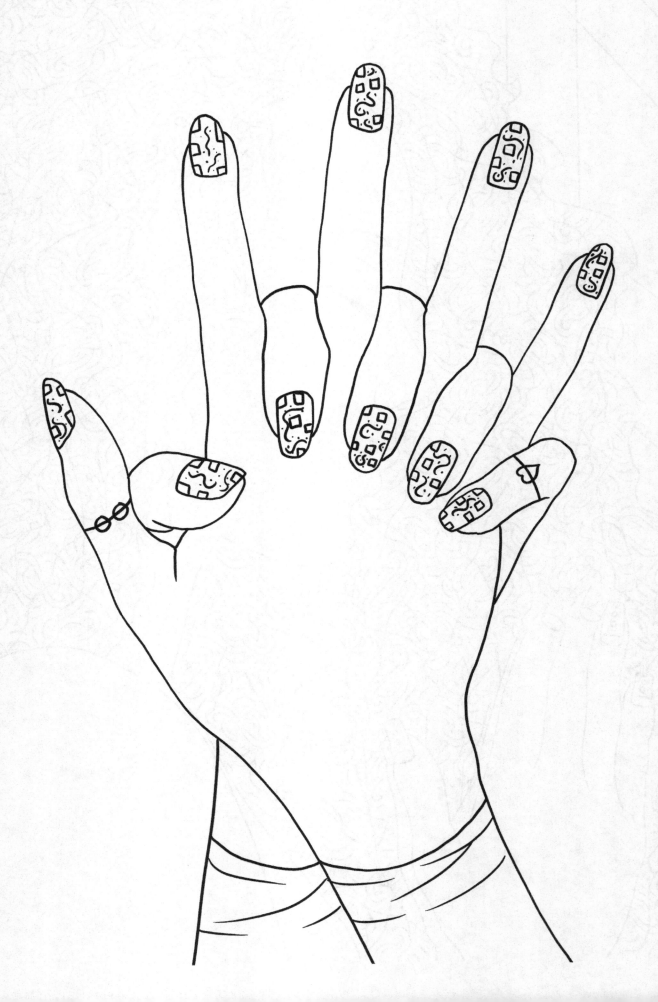

I am not what
Happened to
me, I'm what I
choose
To be.

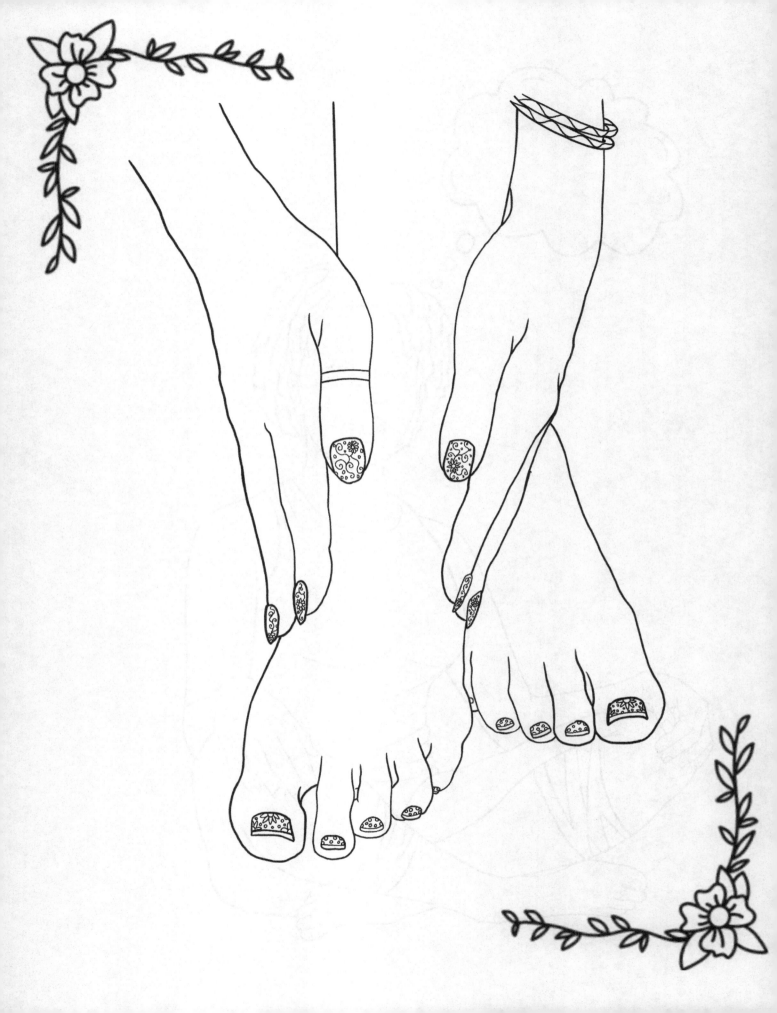

Be Kind To Yourself

Summer

Notes _____

Kids gone
Prayers done
Time for WINE!

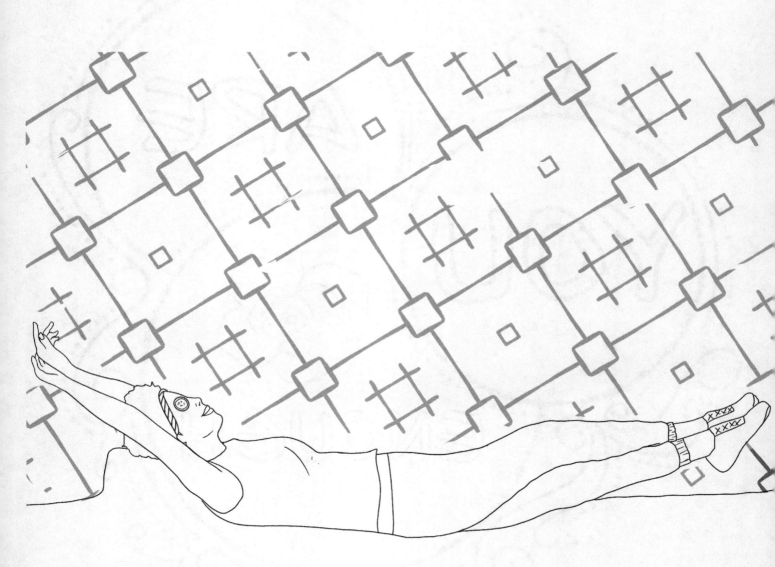

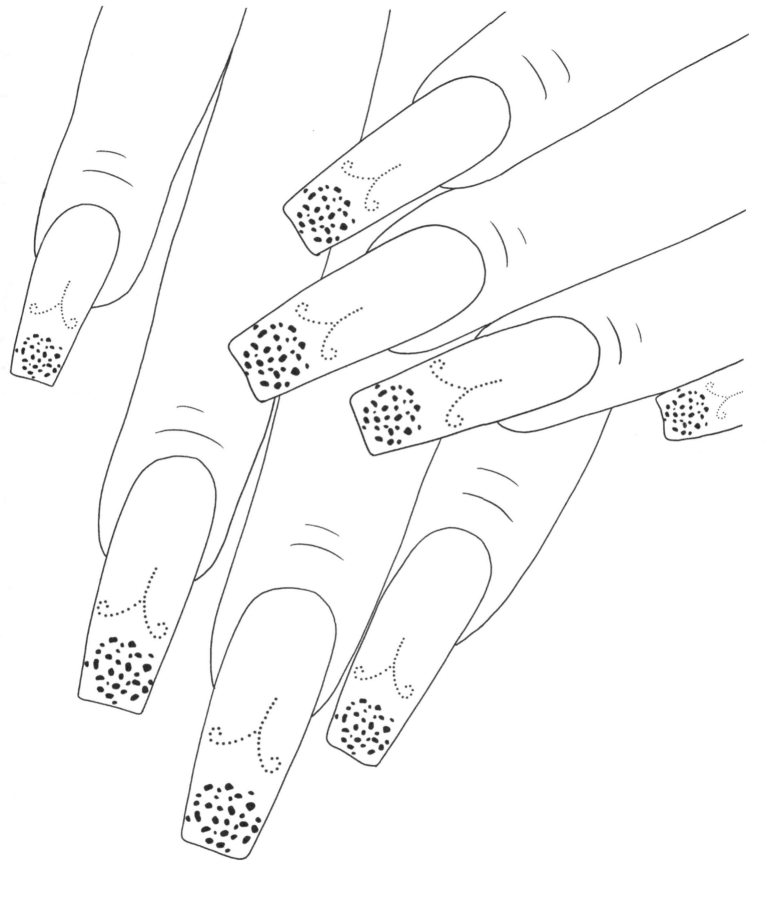

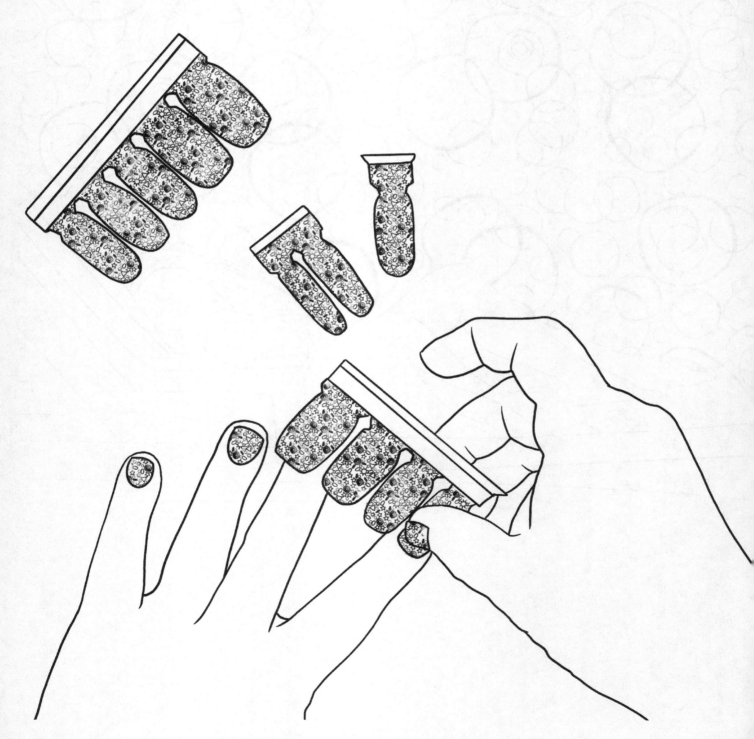

Me Time

Relax

Bond

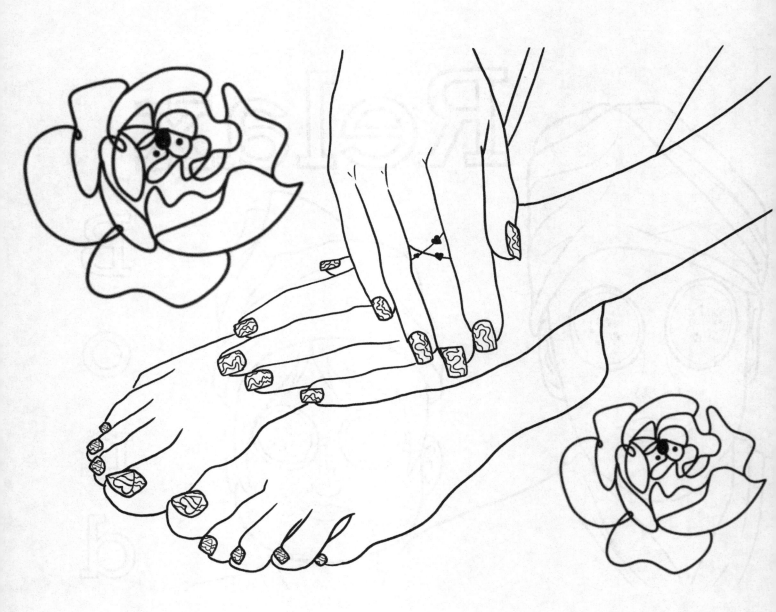

Your Only
Limit Is
Your Mind

About UnwineSelfcare.com

Hello There! Miracle Sims here!

Throughout my life, I've struggled with the idea of taking care of myself. Part of me wants to be the kind of woman that keeps herself up, but more often than not I tend to sacrifice pampering myself for my goals and dreams.

Since I became a mother, I find that the idea of having a little "me time" is very rare... Therefore, I realized that I needed to be more intentional about taking time to "unwine"! After a few embarrassing, and uncomfortable moments of trying to publicly balance motherhood and self-care. For example: Going to the nail salon with my son in his stroller wasn't the relaxing experience that I hoped it would be.

I decided that it was best for me to take matters into my own hands to do what I could to take care of myself, pamper myself, and enjoy a glass of artisan wine all in the comforts of my home!

In the process, I ended up launching two direct sales work-from-home businesses! Miracle of Wine (powered through Wine Shop at Home), and Color Street!

These two businesses combined are what I call Unwine: Self-Care and Sips Spa!

The great thing about Miracle of Wine is that you can join the wine club, and try new wines every month and there are so many gift options for any occasion!

The great thing about Color Street is that you don't have to have great nail painting precision, and there's is no nail drying wait time!

Both can be ordered from the comforts of home, and delivered directly to you!

Scan the QR code below to join our Facebook Group for Daily Interaction, Specials, Giveaways, and More!

*Special Thanks to the amalzing Ammie Govers for bringing my vision to life by creating these beautiful with her illustrations and the wonderful Muhammad Arsal Shaikh for being the editor of my dreams!

But wait there's more!

Coloring Book Challenge:

Color the miracleofwine.com color page, Share it on

social media, and Tag @actressmiraclesims

for $10 off a virtual wine tasting

experience with Miracle Sims!

*Not available in all locations! Contact Miracle for confirmation!

"The name "Miracle of Wine" was inspired by the first miracle as mentioned in John 2:11 and my nickname" -Miracle Sims

What Jesus did here in Cana of Galilee was the first of the signs through which he revealed his glory, and his disciples believed in him.

John 2:11 New International Version (NIV)

On February 8, 2020, Miracle decided to relaunch her wine business Miracle of Wine as an enhancement to her entertainment business Miracle Plays.
However, Since the pandemic, she has created opportunities to wine shop at home by hosting
virtual wine tastings and other experiences!

Visit miracleofwine.com and contact Miracle
for more information about her Wine Business,
and for $5 off of a virtual wine tasting with her!

*Virtual Wine Tasting Experience
May Not Available in All Locations.
(Please contact Miracle to confirm
if this service is available in your area.)

Made in the USA
Columbia, SC
13 December 2024

48035029R00030